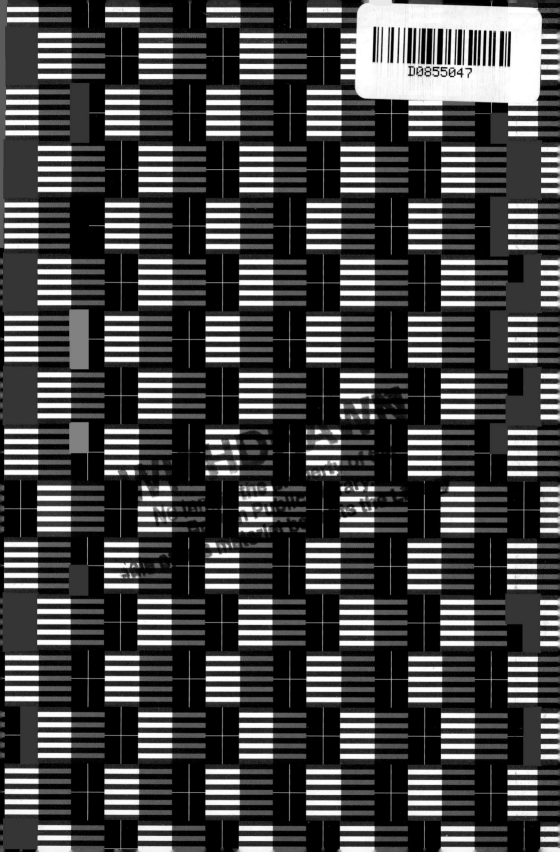

D0855047

WHO YOU ARE
IS WHAT YOU DO

Making choices about life after school

Heather McAllister

WILKINS *farago*

This book is dedicated to Sally Greer with heartfelt thanks
for believing in this project and bringing it to fruition.

And to Janet, Andrew and Robert, my children, whose ongoing
choices about their lives and careers continue to inspire me.

First published in Australia in 2012 by
Wilkins Farago Pty Ltd (ABN 14 081 592 770)
PO Box 78, Albert Park, Victoria 3206, Australia
www.wilkinsfarago.com.au

First published by Beatnik Publishing, Auckland, New Zealand
© Copyright 2010 Heather McAllister
Design © Copyright Beatnik Publishing 2010

National Library of Australia Cataloguing-in-Publication entry

Author:	McAllister, Heather.
Title:	Who you are is what you do: making choices about life after school
	/Heather McAllister.
ISBN:	9780980607024 (hbk.)
Target Audience:	For secondary school age.
Subjects:	Youth–Life skills guides.
	Youth–Vocational guidance.
	Youth–Employment.
	Job hunting–Juvenile literature.
Dewey Number:	305.235
Printed by:	Everbest Printing in China
Distributed by:	Dennis Jones & Associates (Australia),
	Trafalgar Square Books/IPG (United States)

Contents

Welcome to Your Future

I wish I'd had this brilliant little book when I was preparing to leave school.

Ending school can be one of the most daunting experiences of our lives, unless you're in the minority who know exactly what they want to do and have the means to get there.

Your head is full of questions: are there jobs out there for someone like me? Should I study further or just get a job? What about a gap year? What kind of work would I actually enjoy? What if I get stuck in a job or course I hate? What if my school grades aren't good enough to get me the course or job I want?

By helping thousands of kids answer these questions, Heather McAllister has come to the conclusion that the answers aren't going to be found on job websites or in careers guides. The answers are inside us already. Get to know yourself first, she suggests—what your strengths are, what makes you happy, what inspires you, what your values are—and all the other answers will surely follow.

Straight-talking, jargon-free, good-looking, this book is about the big stuff: what kind of person you are, what you believe, what you want out of life. Its canny exercises are designed to draw out what you're suited to and what suits you, and give you the confidence to make the decisions in your own life.

This is also a book for the new generation of school leavers. As Heather says, the days of having a job for life with a single company are well and truly over, and that's changed the way we train for work, the kinds of jobs available and also how we work throughout our lives. Fortunately, it means more options and opportunities than ever before, and chances to take new directions and acquire new skills and interests.

Douglas Adam's legendary Hitchhiker's Guide to the Galaxy had two simple but reassuring words on its front cover: Don't Panic. If you take one message from this book, that's not a bad one. There's no rush. Some careers take more time than others to build and you may change careers several times in your life. So enjoy the journey.

Good books empower people and I hope this book empowers you. Finding a vocation that makes life worthwhile is a noble quest. Good luck on your journey.

Andrew Wilkins
Publisher
Wilkins Farago

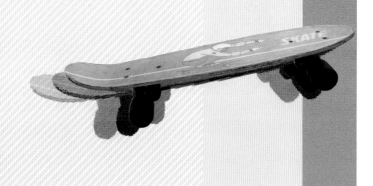

MORE THAN EVER BEFORE

YOUR CAREER CHOICES WILL DEPEND ON

WHO YOU ARE!

Introduction

Understanding what jobs and employers are out there is of course important, but the most important factor in career development today is knowing yourself.

This book will explain why this is important by looking at what having a career means in the 21st century, and how a career now is different from what it was 30, 20 or even 10 years ago.

Although we talk about careers, the main focus of this book will be on you.

To help you find out about yourself, we will look at the ideas of three famous philosophers: Friedrich Nietzsche, Martin Heidegger and Jean-Paul Sartre. They had some interesting and useful thoughts about self-knowledge and what it means to be true to yourself.

Using their ideas I have formulated questions to help you know yourself better – the answers are different for everybody. This book includes blank spaces for you to write down your own answers.

Have a look at your responses a day or two after you've written them. You may also find it interesting to re-read these notes in a few years time. They'll remind you of who you were when you wrote them, and show just how much you've changed and developed since!

I have asked myself these questions several times over the years, as I've changed and as my career has changed. I started work as a teacher when I was just 18, but gained an MA in philosophy in my forties, and have worked in various fields since, including recruitment, philosophical counselling and student liaison. 'Student liaison' means explaining how tertiary institutions such as universities or colleges work and giving advice to students about how to choose the right qualification for themselves.

Much of this book is inspired by my discussions with thousands of students around the country about their life goals and dreams.

I am indebted to them all for this inspiration.

Heather McAllister

CONGRATULATIONS

YOU SURVIVED SECONDARY SCHOOL!

So what are you going to do now?

There are now more opportunities and options than ever before for school leavers – which is both exciting and daunting!

YOU COULD START A COURSE OF STUDY...

No matter where you are there are hundreds of tertiary education institutions – places where you can study or train after secondary school – such as universities, colleges, and private training establishments. They offer thousands of programmes of study.

THERE ARE ALSO OTHER OPPORTUNITIES:

- To find a job immediately after school
- In apprenticeships, such as welding, plumbing, building or cheffing
- In armed forces: the navy, army or airforce
- To travel – do the big gap year

IN A NUTSHELL...HERE ARE THE OPTIONS:

College

UNIVERSITY

ARMED FORCES

Private Training Provider

Apprenticeship

Gap year

Job

HOW ON EARTH ARE YOU GOING TO CHOOSE?

DON'T PANIC!

BELIEVE IT OR NOT, YOU HAVE THE ANSWER ALREADY – YOU JUST MAY NOT RECOGNISE IT YET!

WHERE DO YOU FIT?

Students generally fall into one of three categories when in their final year of school:

1. I know what I want to do when I leave school, and I know what course to take.

2. I have strengths in certain areas but apart from that, I don't really know what I want to do.

3. I have no idea what I want to do when I leave school.

In my experience, most students fall into the second category with about 10% in each of the first and third – in other words, most students feel a bit uncertain about what they want to do when they leave school, even in their final year – even towards the **end** of their final year.

So.........if you are feeling somewhat confused, or even daunted and scared, then you're NOT ALONE – most students are right there in the same boat.

THREE THINGS TO REMEMBER

1 DON'T PANIC – with a bit of help, you'll know the first step to take by the time you finish school – and the first step is all you need.

2 Confusion and uncertainty are part of the decision-making process – it's normal!!

3 Deciding on a career is a process that takes time – there are no instant answers so don't pressure yourself to make a decision before you are ready.

If you read on, you will find some ways to make decisions about your future.

More than ever before, your career choices will depend on **who you are.**

?

BEFORE YOU BEGIN...

CAREERS:
THEN AND NOW

When your parents and caregivers left school, things were very different. The job market has changed over the last few years. These days, we have a lot more control over our futures.

HOW WAS IT DIFFERENT?

When I left school – back in the dark ages of the late 1960s! – girls only had a few options, such as teaching, nursing, secretarial work and serving in a shop.

I chose primary school teaching and expected to teach until I married and had a family. At that time, **most women chose to stay home and raise their children.**

And for **boys?** Well, they had more options than girls but once they had chosen their job, **they were expected to work in that career until they retired**, in order to support their families. They needed to be in a well-paid job, as the burden of paying the mortgage or rent and the bills for food, clothing, power, water and so on generally fell on them. In fact, men were often paid more than women for the same job. The reason given was that they carried more financial responsibility.

It sounds unfair, but values were different then. **Security and permanence were important** to consider when choosing a job, especially for men. The prospect of long-term employment with one employer provided that security.

Companies and institutions controlled their employees' destinies – the job descriptions, the salaries and the retirement benefits. **They were like 'big brother' watching over the workers.** Employees who worked hard for the company were rewarded with promotion or a salary rise. The idea was that if you were loyal to the company, the company would be loyal to you.

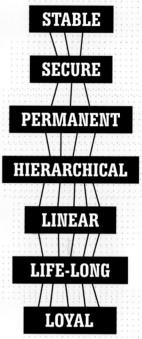

WORDS LINKED TO CAREERS THEN...

WHAT WERE CAREERS THEN?

Careers were something you chose when you left school and continued for the rest of your life – like a long pathway you followed until you retired. You worked your way up the ladder to the top of the hierarchy if you could. All employees worked towards achieving what the company wanted – their personal goals were secondary to the company's.

This is how some parents and grandparents still view a career.
They want you to have security and stability in your life and they feel that the way to achieve this is to follow traditional pathways. You can understand why they might feel that way – it is what was considered best when they were choosing careers.

WHAT ARE CAREERS ABOUT NOW?

These days, we have a lot more control over our futures. There are so many more options – information technology alone has created hundreds of different types of jobs.

We can now focus on our own career goals – we are not dependent on one company to provide us with a life-long career path.

We work towards achieving our goals by moving on to wherever there is a good opportunity to improve our skills.

The responsibility for our development has shifted very much to ourselves – what do I want and where do I want to be?

So it helps to be proactive, even entrepreneurial, and grasp opportunities as they come our way – or even make our own.

It also helps to be good communicators and keep in contact with people we meet along the way.

And it helps to be mobile and flexible.

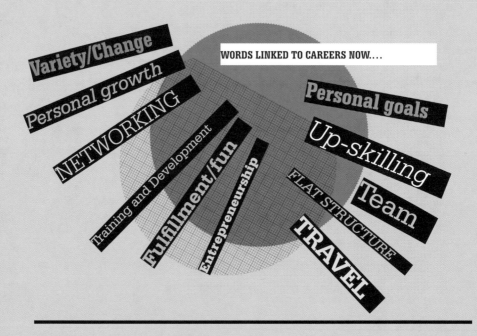

WORDS LINKED TO CAREERS NOW....

Variety/Change
Personal growth
NETWORKING
Training and Development
Fulfilment/fun
Entrepreneurship
Personal goals
Up-skilling
Team
FLAT STRUCTURE
TRAVEL

MY FATHER'S STORY

My father trained as a teacher after World War II. Over the years he worked at several schools, **gradually working his way up the ladder** from teacher to head of the science department. He then went to India to teach and eventually became principal of an international school there. Later, he took a job as the executive officer at another school. His whole career was in education.

MY SON'S STORY

When my son, Rob, left school, he spent the first summer as a surf life-saver. The following year he went down to the Viaduct Basin in Auckland and persuaded the crew of two tourist racing yachts to take him on by promising to work for two weeks without being paid. After the two weeks were up, they offered him a job, which he continued for the rest of the year.

Rob heard that he could make quite a lot of money crewing on superyachts so he gained the qualifications he needed, such as getting a radio licence, and then flew to the Mediterranean and had a job within 24 hours. He returned home after 18 months and with his superyacht savings he bought a house to rent out and invested some money in the share market.

He also enrolled in a Bachelor of Engineering degree which he has just finished. Rob plans to become the CEO of a company, not necessarily in engineering. He has heard that over half of all CEOs in the UK are engineering graduates. Engineers have good problem-solving skills and so are often very successful business managers. In fact, over 50% of people working in business consultancies are also engineering graduates.

So far, Rob's short career is typical of how careers are today: flexible, self-starting, varied, fun and involving continual upskilling.

My father's career is typical of how careers were two generations ago: linear, hierarchical, stable and life-long. Both he and Rob have found fulfillment in what they do – but in different ways.

CAREERS	THEN		CAREERS	NOW
	PERMANENT		CHANGING	
	SECURE		FREE	
	LIFE-LONG		SHORT TERM	
HIERARCHICAL			FLAT STRUCTURED	
	ONE PATHWAY		MULTIPLE PATHWAYS	
	LOYALTY		PERSONAL ADVANCEMENT	
COMPANY GROWTH			PERSONAL GROWTH	

So **now**, careers are about:

YOUR GOALS

YOUR DREAMS

YOUR ASPIRATIONS

As you can see, career choice is now not just one decision leading to a life-long career but a lifetime full of choices and decisions leading to several, sometimes overlapping paths. As you move from role to role gathering the skills you need to achieve your goals, you will be constantly making decisions and looking for the next step.

So, the good news for you here is, you only need to decide the first step!

You only need to have a plan you think is worth trying out for next year, or even the next few months.

As you go on, you will have plenty of scope to change your mind and try different things. As you grow, develop and change, your goals and dreams may develop and change as well.

Everyone's path twists and turns differently.

SERIAL CAREERS

Ian, 37, trained as a lawyer and worked in commercial law, but also used his law knowledge and entrepreneurial skills to set up an insurance business. After five years, he sold the business and he now supports himself by working part-time as a legal adviser. That leaves him enough free time to seriously pursue his current passion – acting.

NEWSREADER TO NEWS MAKER

Katie had always wanted to be a television presenter, so chose to do a communications course. But during her study, she learned about PR – public relations – and it had more appeal. Now, at only 26, she is a publicist for a large company and is in charge of promoting several of their projects in the media.

BEFORE YOU BEGIN...

WHAT SKILLS WILL YOU NEED IN THE WORLD OF WORK?

Here are some of the skills and attributes that your future employers will be looking for.

- Transferable Skills
- Ability to Communicate
- Ability to Take Initiative
- Self-Motivation
- Flexibility

Two examples of **transferable skills** are the ability to be well organised and to have good time management. These skills are important in any work environment.

You **take initiative** when you see what needs doing and do it without being told, or when you think of an easier or more efficient way of doing things and act on it.

Self-motivation is having the desire and discipline to get things done without needing somebody else to watch over you to make sure you do it.

Being **flexible** and **adaptable** means that you can change the way you work as circumstances change, and it means you're willing to change your plans if necessary.

Personal development involves taking opportunities to develop new skills and attributes that help you maintain good relationships, achieve your goals and develop wisdom.

Good **thinking skills** enable you to analyse, judge and problem-solve and to improve ways of doing things.

Computer skills are essential – no business can run efficiently without people who have the skills to use the internet, email and commonly used office software.

Life-long learning is also essential because knowledge is developing so quickly that what you learned even one year ago could now be out of date.

- Commitment to Personal Development
- Thinking Skills
- Computer Literacy
- Life-Long Learning Ability

TEACHER IN DEMAND

Catherine graduated with a Bachelor of Arts and then trained as a history teacher, but after 12 years of teaching, she wanted a change. An employment agency told her the corporate world was hungry for the skills she had developed in teaching: communication and presentation, management, mediation and organisation. With these skills she could train employees. She also found that having studied psychology during her BA was a plus, as it meant she knew how to interpret psychometric testing, which many companies use to assess the personalities of their potential employees.

Catherine joined the Human Resources department of a large multi-national corporation which paid for her to do further study on psychometric testing. She became a very successful trainer and was in demand as the company's Australasian expert on psychometric testing, before setting up her own training consultancy.

IN A NUTSHELL....

Your career won't be a set pathway – in fact, rather than a journey, you could view it as a big jigsaw puzzle where you put in the bits as they come to hand. At the end of your career, there is a full and colourful picture and of course, every picture tells a story.

You may have many changes of job; as your life changes, what you look for in a job may change. While you are young, you may want to travel a lot – you may want change and excitement in your career. Whereas later, you may want to raise a family and so find a more stable job for a few years.

Your career is your story. You can write into your story all the dreams, goals and plans that you are prepared to work for. Like all interesting stories, there will be twists and turns. There will be events and situations that you cannot control and other times when you make important decisions that change the whole course of the tale.

Start thinking about how you'd like to write your story now.

SOME QUESTIONS TO HELP:

What careers do your parents/guardians/grandparents have?

How did they get to where they are now?

At this point, what is the kind of career you would most like to have? In your wildest dreams?

Write a short autobiography of your life so far, but do it in the third person as though you were writing about someone else. Write about where you live, your family and friends, about what you like to do, what you have enjoyed and anything that is important to you.

THIS IS YOUR STORY — IT IS ONGOING. READ IT BACK IN A FEW DAYS. YOU MAY FIND THAT YOU LEARN SOMETHING ABOUT YOURSELF.

SO WHERE DO I BEGIN?

YOU BEGIN WITH YOURSELF!

IT'S ALL ABOUT YOU

You are the one who is responsible
for your career, for your story.
So the big question is then:

WHO AM I?

How do you know who you are?
How do you know what you want
and what makes you happy?

For several years I studied philosophy because
I found these questions really interesting and
many philosophers over the centuries have tried to
answer them. What they say may help you too.

THE THREE PHILOSOPHERS WE LOOK AT IN THIS BOOK:

- Friedrich Nietzsche, who says we are our passions – those strong drives that motivate us, such as wanting to excel.

- Martin Heidegger, who says we are the values that we choose – our priorities and those things that are important to us, such as fairness, family, independence.

- Jean-Paul Sartre, who says we are what we choose. Each decision we make – whether it is about the food we eat or the friends we have – is who we are at that moment.

IT'S ALL ABOUT YOU

F·N
[ne-cha]

FRIEDRICH NIETZSCHE'S ACCOUNT

YOU ARE YOUR PASSIONS

Friedrich Nietzsche, a German, was one of the most controversial philosophers of the 19th century. His philosophy is very complex – at times brilliant and at times difficult to understand. Many of his thoughts are interesting and insightful. You may have heard of one of Nietzsche's sayings:

"What does not destroy me makes me stronger".

THINK/DREAM ABOUT WHERE YOU WOULD LIKE TO BE IN FIVE YEARS TIME.

WHERE WOULD I BE?
WHAT WOULD I BE DOING?

Running your own business? Teaching a class of 6-yearolds?
Climbing the corporate ladder and working in a luxury office downtown?
Making a research breakthrough in climate change or cancer
cures? Working in the music industry as a technician?

NOTE: Put aside all obstacles to that dream and be as over the top and extravagant as you want. Maybe you have made the greatest scientific discovery for the year, maybe you are the youngest cabinet minister on record, maybe you have just won a medal as an athlete in the next Commonwealth Games.

Think about all the times in your life when you have been really happy. Where were you and what were you doing?

_____

_____

_____

_____

_____

_____

_____

_____

Think about what makes you excited. What do you love doing? What do you look forward to when you wake up? What events or things do you look forward to for days beforehand?

_____

_____

_____

_____

_____

_____

_____

_____

THE ANSWERS TO THESE QUESTIONS TELL US ABOUT OUR PASSIONS.

We are our passions

Nietzsche believed that we are our passions. They are the drivers that keep us moving on.

Note that 'passion' in this sense doesn't necessarily mean a strong rush of emotion – not many of us feel like that all the time! So if you simply feel quietly enthusiastic about something rather than wanting to make a big song and dance about it, that can be a 'passion' as well.

Nietzsche's writing could be interpreted this way:

Life is not just about mere survival, but is about becoming stronger, more creative and overcoming the tendencies in ourselves to settle for what is mediocre, uninteresting and boring. Nietzsche calls this creative approach 'becoming'.

An example? **Hanging around feeling bored and not making the effort to do something is giving in to mediocrity.** Whereas working to improve your skills in music or sport, having a great conversation, completing a project, having fun with friends, or reading a great book is motivating and often exciting – it is 'becoming'.

Nietzsche contrasts 'becoming' with what he calls 'being'. 'Being', for Nietzsche, means failing to take on the challenges that life brings us – it's about opting for the path of least resistance and letting life slip by while we fill our time with nothing. We are not really living – we are just existing.

Nietzsche talks about 'wretched contentment' – just settling for the same life as everyone else – in other words: conforming without thinking about what we're doing. To deny your passions, what motivates you, and to choose mediocrity is to deny yourself as a human being and miss out on some great experiences.

> To 'become' is to live life to the full – to be creative in everything we do, to take risks and face challenges with courage, to live life with passion.

CAN'T GET NO SATISFACTION

David was good at physics and did a degree in civil engineering, but he didn't particularly enjoy it. Rather than doing what was expected – getting a job as an engineer – he decided not to do work that gave him no satisfaction. Instead of settling for just 'being' he chose to 'become' by doing what really fascinated him – a social work degree. This led to a long career as a probation officer in criminal rehabilitation; David found fulfillment in helping people get back on the right track. But he also developed another passion – playing the piano. When he was 57, he went back to university to study music and now, three years later, he earns money as a jazz musician.

TO BE CREATIVE CAN MEAN:

being curious about the world

doing an assignment well

having new ideas, taking initiative, thinking for yourself

developing a website

seeing what is being done and improving on it

BOSS PAYS FOR BOOST

Mike struggled with some subjects at school but gained good grades in areas such as technology that were really 'hands-on'. When he left school, he worked for a year, first at a petrol station and then for a welding firm, doing the practical work he liked. His employers were so impressed with his attitude and the way he operated that they offered to pay his fees to do a college course in welding. Because he really enjoyed the course and was technically very skilful, he came top of his class. That gave him the confidence boost to think about setting up his own business. He is now signing up for a Diploma of Business to give him the kinds of skills he will need to run his own company.

WHAT DOES 'BECOMING' MEAN FOR US?

To become is to be open to new ideas, new actions, new ways of thinking, new possibilities for change.

To become is to overcome hurdles that get in the way of our dreams; to have the nerve to move on instead of staying in our 'comfort zone'.

To become and to overcome is to accept the difficult times as an opportunity to become stronger, not an excuse to opt out. In other words, when things are tough, you face the situation. Whether it is difficult school work or an argument with your brother or sister, if you work it out rather than running away, you will be stronger for the experience.

To become is to open yourself to change, to not resist it but embrace it and learn from it. No excuses for avoiding new challenges!

achieving the goals that inspire you

trying out new tactics in sport — solving a mathematical problem

thinking up a new way of organising an event

OPPORTUNITIES

Think about interesting opportunities you've had that you turned down because you were afraid, didn't think you could make it or couldn't be bothered. Now think of any decision you've made where you've chosen a more challenging option because it was potentially more fulfilling instead of settling for the easiest option. How did it work out? Would you do the same again?

If you don't take the exciting opportunities that cross your path, you may miss out on something that will bring you great fulfilment.

To give in to your fears, doubts and inertia is to settle for mediocrity. Mediocrity is not very satisfying. It leads to boredom and lack of motivation which in turn can lead to restlessness and depression.

If you are enjoying what you do it will energise you and others around you. **Grasp those possibilities, face those fears, act on those ideas you have.**

DON'T GIVE UP HOPE

Sienna really wanted to be a chef so she applied for two courses. The first – at a college – looked as though it would suit her down to the ground, and the second – a private training provider (PTP) – was her back-up plan. She was immediately accepted into the PTP but missed out on the college course by a few places and was put on the waiting list. Disappointed but determined, Sienna called the college every week over the summer to see if anybody had pulled out of the course. The answer was always 'no' and Sienna started going to the PTP course; which began a week earlier than the college course. But just when all hope seemed lost, she finally got the call telling her the college had a place free, and she transferred to where she wanted to be. Her passion for creating amazing food motivated her not to settle for anything less than what she really wanted.

WHAT MOTIVATES YOU?

Now look at your answers to the questions on the Nietzsche Food for Thought pages (27-28). What are your dreams or aspirations for your future? **Look at your dreams and goals carefully because they reveal what you are passionate about, what motivates you and makes life interesting.**

Sometimes we enjoy a subject because the teacher is really enthusiastic about it and his or her enthusiasm is contagious. If you really like what you do – as these teachers do – you will probably do well, if you are prepared to put the work in and face the challenges. **Then your creativity can take flight.**

FROM PLUMBER TO LECTURER

Justin found school tough and decided to leave at the end of Year 11/5th Form. He found work as a plumber's assistant and while the job was ok, he didn't really enjoy it. His thoughts drifted back to interesting ideas he'd learned in Classical Studies – he had had a very inspirational teacher and the subject had fascinated him. He discovered that he could learn a lot more about ancient history and classics at university so he bravely applied to do a Bachelor of Arts in Classics. He was admitted because he had completed Year 11/5th Form, he had fulfilled the requirements for Mature Entry and he was very motivated to study. Justin went on to gain good marks in his degree and is now planning to become a lecturer.

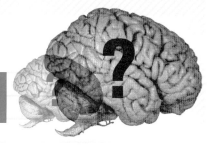

SOME MORE QUESTIONS TO DETERMINE YOUR MOTIVATIONS:

What are all the people, places, subjects, sports, music, books and websites that you like, that you enjoy and appreciate? Write down what makes you feel the most enthusiastic.

What activities 'bring you to life'? It may be playing a sport or writing a poem or climbing mountains. Or it may be chilling out with a group of friends. It may be acting or making people laugh.

How do you use your creativity? Think about something you created and how you felt about it.

What are all the dreams you have had over the years about what you might do with your life? What would you most like to create? Is there anything you have seen or experienced where you thought, "I wish I could do that"?

Now stop and reflect on your answers. Do you see some clues within them as to what you are really interested in and what motivates you?

What gives you a sense of achievement? For some people it is winning a race, or completing a difficult assignment; for others it is mastering a musical instrument and for some it is listening to a friend's problem and making them feel a little better. Each person rates achievement by how it affects them personally – and we're all different.

What are your strengths? We usually excel in the areas we are strongest in. Think about the things you do well.

Your strengths might include:
- those subjects at school where you get good grades
- the sports you're involved in
- a musical instrument you play
- art - as in painting, photography, sculpture, design, fashion
- organising or getting people to work together
- working well with children

You might be good at:
- rugby
- acting
- singing
- communicating
- making things and fixing things

You might be the sort of person everyone relies on at a time of crisis. Write about your strengths. If you are having trouble thinking of what they are, ask family members, a good friend and/or a trusted teacher.

IMPORTANT TIPS

- Grasp every opportunity you can to grow stronger and face hurdles with determination, with what Nietzsche calls a resounding "Yes!"

- Set goals that suit your creativity, strengths and motivations, and work out the steps to achieve those goals. Each step you take brings you closer to achievement.

- Have a positive attitude towards struggles along the way.

- Don't let discouragement stop you from moving on.

- Be an overcomer.

- Don't settle for mediocrity.

IMPORTANT POINTS

- Friedrich Nietzsche says we are our passions or drivers.

- Keywords for his definition of what it means to be passionate are: becoming, creating, overcoming.

- Facing life with an affirming attitude is healthy – "What does not destroy you makes you strong".

- Settling for mediocrity is inauthentic and can lead to restlessness and depression.

- Discover your creative self.

- Discover your strengths.

- Think about the possibilities for your life and the dreams you have.

It only takes one step at a time to achieve your goals. One of the hurdles we face is being daunted – thinking we'll never make it. If you only take one step at a time, it's easy. It may be as simple as filling in an application form and sending it off.

To be creative is to be yourself.

We are our passions, our creativity, our dreams and our strengths.

IT'S ALL ABOUT YOU

M. Heidegger [hi-de-gar]

MARTIN HEIDEGGER'S ACCOUNT

YOU ARE WHAT YOU VALUE

Martin Heidegger was a German philosopher who lived in the 20th century, a generation or so after Nietzsche. He believed that to really be yourself, you have to stop conforming to what everyone else says and work out how you want to live and what you want to do – in other words, work out what you think is important and what you value highly.

But he also believed that you can't be yourself in a vacuum! You live with people and so you show who you are by the way you relate to others and to your environment. He didn't think you could know yourself by looking inwards but by looking at how you interact with people and the world around you.

THINK ABOUT WHAT IS IMPORTANT TO YOU.

What do you think are your most important character traits? Honesty, integrity, independence,adventurousness, kindness?

Do you value friends? If so, what do you expect from your friends – fun, loyalty, action, sharing, honesty? Chances are that what you expect from a friend is what you find important for yourself.

Is family important to you? Religion? What are the things or people you value and admire the most? What could you do without in life?

WHAT COULD YOU NOT LIVE WITHOUT?

FOLLOWING WHAT 'THEY' SAY

Heidegger believed that at first, we unconsciously look to those around us to find out how to live. We also look to them for approval. We unconsciously accept that the way to live is how they live. **We change ourselves to fit the image we think others expect of us.** Often you hear such statements as 'They will laugh at me if I do this', or 'They will think I am stupid if I say this', or 'If I don't do this, they will notice'.

IS WHAT 'THEY' EXPECT THE ONLY WAY?

Heidegger says that in conforming to the 'they' without really thinking about what we are doing we are not being true to ourselves. Have you seen other people doing really stupid things to be accepted into a clique, group or gang?

Have you found yourself laughing at someone because everyone else is, even though you don't really want to?

Heidegger says that we are conforming to the 'they' when we do those things.

FORGET THE 'THEY' – BE YOURSELF

So how do we come to a place where we challenge the 'they' and really become ourselves? Heidegger says that it happens when you consciously realise that you're not going to live forever, that you are eventually going to die. Knowing that life is finite, and you only have one 'crack' at it, spurs you on to think about what you want to achieve and also makes you think about the meaning of your life and what you value. Because our lives have an end, time is precious, and it makes sense to fill our allocation of time with things that are important to us, and not waste it on things we think aren't so important.

Once you understand this, you stop trying to be a clone, conforming to what your peers or 'they' expect of you. **Who wants to get to the end of their lives and realise they have spent it trying to meet other people's expectations and missing out on the life they would really like to have lived?**

Heidegger believed that once we recognise this and begin choosing our own lives, we are being true to ourselves. We can then live in a way that is meaningful to us, not just blindly conform to what 'they' say.

BEING OURSELVES IN OUR COMMUNITY

This does not mean we ignore those around us. Because we live in community, we also need to take into consideration how our choices affect others. Although what 'they' say is superficial, if we dig down we will find the less superficial values in our community. These may be values such as caring about others and treating them as we would want to be treated ourselves.

TASK:

Think about your community. This includes your family, friends, their families, neighbours, schoolmates, teachers, team-mates, the people who serve you in your local shop, maybe internet groups and church/temple/mosque and anyone else you might see on a regular basis, as well as your MP, mayor and local council.

Ask yourself these questions:
What is important to you and to your community?
What do you expect of them and they of you?

Is honesty important? Do you expect people around you to tell you the truth? Would you expect your friends to always be honest with you? How do you feel about people who lie to you or can't be trusted?

Is loyalty important? When life gets tough, do you expect your friends to 'be there for you' and would you do the same for them? If you got into trouble would you expect them to support you? Would you lie for them or would it be more important to tell the truth?

Is family life important to you and your community?
For instance, do you value the times you spend with other families, socialising and enjoying their company? Do families in your community help each other out in a crisis?

Is religion important to you? If so, how does this affect the way you live?

How are you and your community considerate of each other?
How considerate do you expect them to be and how considerate are you to others?

Does your community value independence? Do your parents and teachers give you much freedom to make your own choices? Do they encourage you to try new activities, travel, take calculated risks? Do you want that independence?

Do you share all of your community's values and the level of importance that is attached to each? Are there any values you hold as well as, or instead of, some of your community's values? Go back and look at the Heidegger Food for Thought (page 39).

Choosing by values

When you are making decisions about what you want to do with your life, **you need to take your values into consideration**. For instance, if you value honesty and respect for others, then you probably won't want to work with people who are dishonest, tell lies and don't treat people with respect. Your expectations would be continually disappointed. Or if you are energetic, efficient and a high achiever, you probably wouldn't enjoy working with a team of people who are just looking forward to their lunch break.

WORKING WITH STRICT GUIDELINES

Some people value rules and regulations highly. They like to work in a place where there are plenty of guidelines and they know exactly what they are allowed to do and not to do. Some people find that kind of workplace too restrictive, so probably would not be happy working there.

If you value independence and don't like working closely with other people on projects, this may indicate that you don't value being part of a team. You may find you prefer to be your own boss and be self-employed.

MY STORY

I worked for a company once who did not respect or care for other people. They did not fulfil promises they made to their clients and they did not pay people who had provided services for them until those people begged them – and then they would pay them only a small percentage of what they owed as long as the creditors promised to provide their services again. I saw people's livelihoods destroyed because of the large debts owed to them by the company I worked for. Because I think it's important to respect people and treat them as I would like to be treated, I found it very difficult to work in that environment. In the end I left and went to work where people respected the rights of others, something I value strongly.

THE PARTY SET

If you value lots of talk and fun, then you need to think about the sorts of jobs and employers who would have a lively environment in which to work. This depends on the culture of the company so it is important that you find out about that when you are applying for a job. There are many companies that value social interaction and encourage their employees to become part of the 'family'. There are other companies where socialising is not so important but where you would be encouraged to get on with the job and keep your social life separate from your work life – which also suits some people.

BEING GREEN

If you are passionate about the environment and value conservation then you may choose to do something where you are able to practice those values. You might want to work for the Department of Sustainability, Environment, Water Population and Communities or an organisation that promotes environmentally friendly activities.

GOING AGAINST THE GRAIN

Josh's father was an architect and his mother a GP. His brother was just completing a law degree and his sister was at medical school. Josh's family expected that he would study for one of these prestigious professions but Josh was not really interested. At school, the subject he liked best was art. He also loved being outdoors and was very interested in ecological sustainability. After discussions with friends and teachers, and some research on the net, Josh decided to do a landscape design course at a college. After some persuasion, his parents accepted that Josh did not want to take the pathway they had planned for him. Josh now has a job with a landscape design company that he enjoys very much.

PROFESSIONAL VALUES

So far, we've talked about basing your choice of employer on your values. Now think about some of the different values people in different professions may have. For instance:

- Lawyer – justice, fairness, supporting others, debate
- Doctor – care for the health and well-being of others, scientific advancement
- Accountant – care of resources, problem-solving
- Dive instructor – adventure, being outdoors
- IT specialist – logical thinking, working individually, problem-solving
- Social worker – welfare of others, social interaction and communication
- Fashion designer – art, creativity, change
- Engineer – problem-solving, logical thinking, being hands-on
- Art gallery curator – art and philosophy, beauty and form

These, of course, are not the only values they hold but without holding those values, then the field they chose may not really suit them. So for instance an IT specialist may also have strong values of justice and fairness or care for the well-being of others but those are not the primary values required for an IT job.

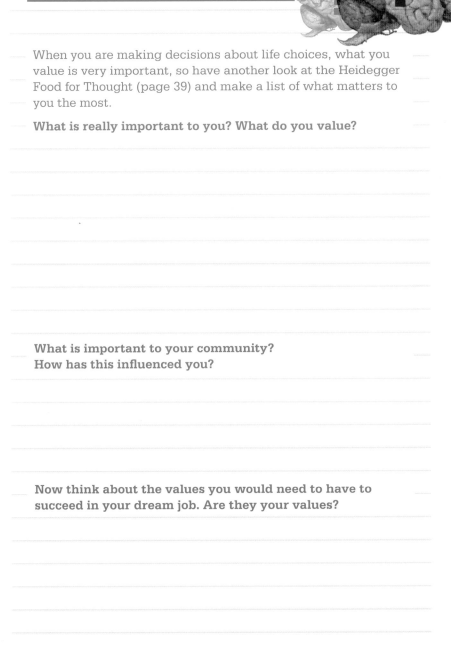

QUESTIONS ABOUT VALUES

When you are making decisions about life choices, what you value is very important, so have another look at the Heidegger Food for Thought (page 39) and make a list of what matters to you the most.

What is really important to you? What do you value?

What is important to your community?
How has this influenced you?

Now think about the values you would need to have to succeed in your dream job. Are they your values?

- Think about what is important to you.

- When you choose an employer, make sure you have similar values.

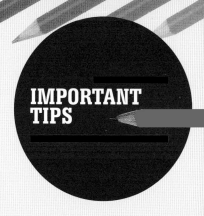

IMPORTANT TIPS

IMPORTANT POINTS

- You are what you value.

- Being yourself is knowing what is important to you, not just following blindly what everyone else does.

- Being yourself involves being part of the community in which you live and the relationship you have with your community.

- Knowing what your values are is useful when choosing where you want to work and who you want to work for.

IT'S ALL ABOUT YOU

Jean-Paul

[sahr-truh]

JEAN-PAUL SARTRE'S ACCOUNT

LIFE AS DECISION MAKING: I AM MY CHOICES

One of the best known philosophers of the mid-twentieth century was a Frenchman, Jean-Paul Sartre.

He believed that:

We are the choices we make – we are our decisions.

WHAT ARE THE IMPORTANT DECISIONS YOU HAVE MADE SO FAR IN YOUR LIFE?

What are some important decisions others have made for you?

WHAT DOES HE MEAN BY "WE ARE OUR CHOICES"?

Sartre thinks that what sets us apart from other living creatures is that, rather than behaving from instinct only, we can think about our decisions. For instance, when you are planning for the weekend, you can think about the options such as playing a game of football, going to the shopping mall, doing homework or hanging out at home. You think about the options and choose between them.

Sartre believes that this ability to think about decisions and weigh up the options is uniquely human and is what defines us. **He believes that what we are is determined by what we choose – we are our freedom to choose.**

Instead of being programmed or having to fit into a pigeonhole, you can decide how to lead your life. **You are the decisions you make, both big and small.**

Sartre also believes that if we deny this ability to think about our decisions, we are being inauthentic. If we believe we are just carried through life as passengers, that we have no say and blame our circumstances for what happens to us, we are not true to ourselves as human beings.

TAKING RESPONSIBILITY FOR OUR CHOICES

Our choices have consequences for our lives. Each of our decisions influences who we are – our choices about the food we eat, our response to others, our friends, our interests and of course, our choices about tertiary education and career. Each individual carries the responsibility for their own choices.

WHO DARES WINS A TRIP TO FRANCE

Janet was awarded a scholarship to go to France. Her friends told her she was very lucky – yet they were all good students with as much chance of gaining the scholarship as she had, but they had chosen not to apply. It was Janet's decision to take that action which eventually led her to winning a scholarship and a great opportunity to travel. It didn't happen by some lucky chance. Her friends made a choice, whether they were aware of it at the time or not, not to apply. When we ignore opportunities, we make a choice – a passive one.

SO WHAT!?

How do we apply that in terms of choosing a career? Think about it. **You are responsible for who you are and what you do. You get to choose!** The possibilities are endless. **Choosing a pathway for your life is exciting!** Think about all the things you would like to do in your life. They may all be possible – you don't have to do them all at once. Some goals may take a long time to achieve and you may find they change along the way. But if you make good decisions, you may achieve all your dreams, some earlier in life, some later.

FLIPSIDE OF RESPONSIBILITY

The flipside to this is that we are also responsible for our decisions. If you make decisions about the future by carefully researching the options available, you will probably make good decisions.

You cannot blame anyone else, however, for unwise choices you make, such as leaving decisions about your future to others.

I know of students who have left it to their mothers to research the possibilities of their future moves. It is their mothers who have filled in the forms and their mothers who have followed up the paper work. When it doesn't work out, whose fault is it? The mothers'? NO! Those students made a decision to leave it to someone else to determine their future. If things don't work out, the responsibility is theirs. That doesn't mean that you don't consult with other people who have more experience than you. You can listen and weigh up the options, but the final decision is yours.

When things don't work out, it is useful to think about why, rather than placing blame. You can learn from mistakes and make new decisions to change things and get better results. **If you make decisions that don't work out, it's not the end of the world.** You may even change your goals along the way.

NO NAME CALLING

To Sartre, nothing about us is fixed. **Has anyone ever told you that you are a lazy person or a failure?** Or do people stereotype you as 'the artist' when you like science just as much as art? Sartre says that labelling you – setting you in concrete – is false or inauthentic. **You may have made decisions or behaved in a certain way in the past but those actions and decisions do not define you forever.** You have the option of choosing other actions that have different outcomes – if you want to.

YOUR VISION FOR YOUR LIFE

Sometimes we receive messages from other people that dampen our visions and dreams. But:

 *your* **life is determined by** *your* **commitment to** *your* **goals.**

It is your decisions that will make things happen. **That's empowering.** You may not have everything in place yet to achieve what you want, but if you set a realistic goal, you can make decisions that will help you achieve it.

You can challenge the messages that you have given yourself or that others have given you such as 'You couldn't do that' or 'You haven't got what it takes'. Check out the possibilities yourself. **Don't rely on what others say to you.**

BEING REAL

It is also important to be realistic about your aspirations. For instance, if your goal is to be a doctor but you don't like science, this might not be a realistic goal. Think about why you want to be a doctor: Is it so you can help people? Is it so you can make money? What are some other careers that help people and/or make money which don't involve so much scientific study?

Or if you want to be a great musician but can't be bothered practising, then think hard because being a good musician takes a lot of self-discipline. You have to be really committed to consider this. Think about the things you do well and enjoy. Do your goals match up with these? **Dreaming and thinking about what you want is just the beginning.**

TAKING CONTROL

The message Jean-Paul Sartre brings to you is: **take control of your life.** Think about what you want to achieve and how you want to live. Do you want to be healthy? Then make good choices about what you eat and how you treat your body. Do you want to have good friends and relationships? Then choose your friends wisely and treat them well. Do you want to have a great life? Then start thinking about what you think a great life would be, dream a little or a lot, and think about the steps toward achieving that life. **The sky is the limit!**

IMPORTANT POINTS

- Jean-Paul Sartre says that you are your freedom to choose.

- Unlike other beings, we as human beings have the ability to think about our decisions. If we ignore this ability we are not being true to ourselves.

- We get to choose what we do and who we become – we are the CEOs of our own lives.

- Even if our goals seem difficult to reach, there are choices we can make that will help us achieve them.

- Our choices have consequences that affect our lives both positively and negatively.

- We must take responsibility for those consequences.

THE MOST IMPORTANT POINT

We have the power to make choices.

IT'S ALL ABOUT YOU

SKILLS

To know yourself fully, another important area to consider is your skills.

As mentioned in the first chapter, the skills required for employment have changed over the years.

Knowledge is changing and developing all the time. Not only is it important to be a good learner, it is also important to be open and flexible; adaptable to new environments and new ways of doing things; and ready to take initiative.

It is also important to know broadly where you want to go and to develop the skills that will take you there.

You are responsible for your own development and if you are self-motivated, you are more likely to achieve your goals.

Now let's look at the skills you have already developed...

TAKE 'ABILITY TO COMMUNICATE'

You will have had opportunities to develop your written communication skills in school, for instance, in your English or History classes.

You may have developed oral communication skills through speech competitions or by reporting back to the class on a project or by being a sports captain and encouraging your team.

You may have helped produce the school yearbook, perhaps developing skills such as editing, proofing, writing and communicating successfully with other contributors in a team project.

You may have taken part in a drama production.

Being able to perform well and express yourself to a large audience is a very useful skill if your job requires public speaking such as teaching or delivering presentations in a business meeting. It builds your confidence too.

ACTION

Think about other ways you have developed good communication skills at school.

TAKE 'ABILITY TO SHOW INITIATIVE'

Have you been involved in events or class activities where you took the lead by making useful suggestions and worked with the others to make things happen?

Are you the sort of person who sees what needs doing and does it without being told?

If you have those skills, you will be valued as an employee in most organisations and you will work well with a team.

You could also be identified as someone who has the potential to become a good manager.

ACTION

Think about something you have done in the last few days that shows your ability to take initiative.

WHAT ABOUT 'SELF-MOTIVATION'?

When was the last time you had a specific goal to achieve? Perhaps you wanted to buy a car or save money for a road trip. Perhaps you really wanted to win the school cross-country or do well in an exam.

How did you achieve that goal?

Did you get a weekend job or get out of bed early to train or study?

When you organised yourself to achieve that goal you were being self-motivated.

Some students understand that if they get good grades at school, this will give them more options, as some courses have higher entry standards than others.

If these students do all they can to achieve good grades, they are being self-motivated.

On the other hand, those students who rely on their parents to cajole and nag them into studying are not self-motivated.

Note: usually motivation comes from a desire to achieve.

GOOD ORGANISATIONAL SKILLS ARE ALSO IMPORTANT

You may have begun to develop these skills at school by being on the school ball committee or by organising sports events.

You may be involved in student government.

You may simply have a busy schedule of school work, sports commitments and family commitments to juggle! None of these experiences are wasted. When you leave school, no matter what your next step, you will need to be well organised if you want to succeed.

If you go to a university or a college, you will have to remember what classes to go to, where they are held, at what time, and when the assignments are due. No one will be chasing you up for your work or making sure you are prepared for your tests and examinations. You have to make sure you attend the right tutorials and diarise in your examination dates.

When you begin working full-time, you will have to be punctual and plan your day so that you can achieve all that is expected.

ACTION

You could begin now, by getting a diary and planning your week so that you have a good balance of work, study, leisure.

GOOD RELATIONSHIP SKILLS ARE ESSENTIAL

You will need them in order to network with others and maintain good customer service.

Don't think that 'customer service' just means someone in a call centre answering phones or in a shop serving customers. Companies these days, from small retail businesses to the largest corporate businesses and legal firms, know the value of looking after clients and getting on well with colleagues.

You practise people skills at school every day, with your friends, your teachers and other school staff.

You will get much further in life if you know how to listen, communicate and relate well with people around you.

The list of skills is endless.

If you are good at mathematics, you may be good at logical thinking and have the ability to problem-solve.

Studying literature also develops good thinking and analytical skills, and a different kind of creativity.

If you are good at science you may have developed skills in noting the details, being precise and drawing conclusions from what you find.

If you are interested in history, you may have developed good research skills and the ability to understand more about your heritage and other people's, and what brings about change.

ACTION

Practise talking to each person you meet as though they are the most interesting person in the world and see what the results are.....
you could be surprised!

ACTION

Now that you have thought about it, write a list of skills that you have had the opportunity to develop while at school. Think of ways those skills might be useful in a job.

ACTION

Think about what you really want to achieve in your life. Write it down and tape it to the mirror. Let that be your motivator.

WHAT NEXT?

PUTTING TOGETHER THE PIECES

SO WHO ARE YOU?

We have now explored several aspects of ourselves – our passions, creativity, strengths, values, dreams, skills and the choices we make.

In order to make wise decisions about the future, you need to take all those aspects into consideration. As you look at all of these together, you may begin to

see the overall picture of yourself.

Check out all the things you've thought about while reading this book: your dreams, goals, strengths, skills, creative talents, interests and values.

Now bring them together and put them side-by-side in the table below. Prioritise the items in each list – put them in order of importance. For instance, at the top of the dreams column, put the dream you most want to achieve. At the top of the skills column, put your strongest skill, and so on.

DREAMS & GOALS	STRENGTHS	CREATIVE TALENTS	INTERESTS	SKILLS	VALUES

**STOP AND LOOK AT THE LISTS.
WHAT ARE YOUR MOST IMPORTANT DREAMS?
STRENGTHS? CREATIVE TALENTS? VALUES?**

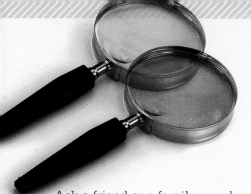

Now look back at the autobiography of yourself.

Ask a friend or a family member to do the same for his or herself. Now swap the 'biographies' with your friend and read them to each other. It may sound strange, but it can give you a more objective view of yourself and it is surprising what you may find out by doing this simple exercise.

Creating pathways to your dreams and goals.

Now that you have a better idea of all that contributes to who you are:

Look at what you have put at the top of your dreams list. Let's say, for example, that your goal is to own your own bookshop.

Now look at what is at the top of your other columns. Do these top priorities fit with your dream? For example, one of your interests may be reading. That would fit in with an interest in books.

Now look at all your strengths. As a bookshop is a financial venture, do you have any strengths in organisation, accounting, economics or anything that relates to running a business? Do you know your way around a spreadsheet? Is this something that you might want to study and develop or is it something you have absolutely no interest in? Remember that business does not have to be your main area of study; you may be able to do a short business course, or take accounting as one of several subjects in a degree.

Most dreams are possible if you are prepared to take the steps towards them – even the seemingly impossible dreams. Determination and commitment to the dream will get you there in the end. Look at those who have achieved great things in their lives – you can be sure the achievement did not happen overnight. Even Einstein worked in a patent office for years before he was recognised as a great genius.

PUTTING TOGETHER THE PIECES

STILL NOT CLEAR?

Having thought about all these aspects of yourself, you may still be unclear as to what to do next. Not everyone has special dreams or aspirations, and for some who are good all-rounders, there are so many possible pathways that it is hard to choose between them. Don't be too concerned if this is the case. Here are some pointers to take into consideration.

1. *THE BETTER THE QUALIFICATION, THE BETTER THE CHANCE OF EARNING WELL.*

We all know about cases where someone without an education has become a multi-millionaire through sheer hard work and determination. **Those are the exceptions.** Statistics show that generally, if you want to earn a lot, then the higher your qualification the higher your potential earnings.

2. *IF YOU ARE NOT SURE WHAT YOU WANT TO DO, CHOOSE A QUALITY TERTIARY INSTITUTION THAT IS WELL-KNOWN AND RESPECTED AND START A WELL-RECOGNISED QUALIFICATION IN AN AREA OR SUBJECT THAT YOU FIND INTERESTING.*

As a rule of thumb, universities are more focussed on research and theory while college courses are usually more vocational – designed to train you for a specific career area or job. There are some exceptions. For instance, to be a doctor, lawyer or professional engineer, you must study at a university. Private Training Providers (PTPs) generally offer niche courses, such as hairdressing, tourism and web design, many of which are well-respected in their industries. **To get an idea of how universities are rated, check out independent assessments** such as the world rankings of universities from the Times Education Supplement from London – go to www.timeshighereducation.co.uk and click on 'Stats'.

3. *IF YOU DON'T GET ACCEPTED INTO THE COURSE OR QUALIFICATION AT THE TOP OF YOUR LIST, DON'T DESPAIR!*

Often you can begin your tertiary study with a starter qualification in the same subject. A certificate or diploma will probably be shorter than a first degree and will increase your chances of getting into your first choice after you've completed it. **This is called 'staircasing' – preliminary qualifications are used as a 'step up'.** Sometimes if you do well in your first qualification, some of the courses in the qualification at the top of your list may be waived and it won't take as long to complete. For instance, a business diploma may qualify you to study further for a business degree at a university, depending on your grades.

STAIRWAY TO DESIGN HEAVEN

Ruby missed out on getting into a university's three-year degree course in design, but was accepted into the year-long certificate course run by the same department. She wasn't the only one – at least 90% of the people wanting to do the degree had to do the certificate first. It was a good taster for everyone as the certificate, like the degree, was more conceptual than a lot of people had expected. The students were able to tell whether they would like doing the degree or not, without committing to three years of study, while also gaining a certificate qualification. Ruby loved it, gained a lot of confidence and went on to do the degree.

COMPUTER NATURAL

Nick was unhappy at school, and against his parents' wishes, left before he had gained any qualification. After doing several very repetitive jobs which led to nothing, he realised that he wasn't going to find employment that satisfied him unless he had some qualifications. With some of the roles he applied for, although he had the skills, others got the job because they had appropriate qualifications. Because he had a natural aptitude for computer programming he applied to do a certificate in computing at a local college. He did not need the same entrance requirements as the diplomas and degrees, and because he showed aptitude and motivation, he was accepted. After successfully completing the certificate, there was no holding back. He went from the certificate to a diploma in computing, and because of his high grade point average he has been accepted into a university degree with a major in computer programming.

4. *YOU CAN KEEP YOUR OPTIONS OPEN ONCE YOU LEAVE SCHOOL BY DOING A BROAD, GENERAL DEGREE LIKE A BACHELOR OF ARTS OR SCIENCE.*

It doesn't matter so much what subject your degree or qualification is in, it is the skills that you develop by studying and the level of the qualification that are important. For instance, if you were to apply for a government job in the Treasury, you might think that applicants would have to have a commerce or business degree. In fact, this is not the case. Generally a Master's degree will be required but Treasury likea to have graduates from a diverse range of subjects such as arts and science. **If you are not sure whether you want to be a teacher or not, you don't have to go straight to a teaching qualification**; you can complete a degree in another subject first, and then if you still want to teach, do a one-year postgraduate diploma in teaching.

5. IF YOU ARE STUDYING FOR A DEGREE, DON'T NARROW DOWN YOUR CHOICES TOO SOON; TAKE THE OPPORTUNITY IN THE FIRST YEAR TO TRY OUT A FEW DIFFERENT SUBJECTS.

It is possible to keep your options open during your first years of tertiary study – you're not locked in and you can change your mind. **Your first year of study can be a time when you try out different subjects** – perhaps some that weren't offered at school – and find out what suits you and what doesn't. Some programmes are very broad at first and you may not even be permitted to specialise until your second year. You might discover something that you really like that will open up other possibilities for you. Some courses can be reassigned into another degree if you change your mind about your entire qualification.

6. SOME STUDENTS PREFER TO GET SOME LIFE EXPERIENCE FIRST BY GOING OVERSEAS FOR A GAP YEAR OR WORKING FOR A TIME TO SAVE MONEY FOR THEIR EDUCATION.

This is a good way of taking a breather from study to do some thinking about your goals. There is nothing like working in a low-paid repetitive job to motivate you to study for a worthwhile qualification!

7. WORKING WHILE STUDYING CAN HELP YOUR CAREER PROSPECTS.

Many tertiary students have part-time jobs, or holiday jobs. After graduation, this can be an advantage as prospective employers will look to see what skills you have gained, not only through study but by having the maturity and organisational skills to hold down a job and succeed in study at the same time. If you have good references from these roles, **they can be very useful for getting a 'foot in the door' for your first full-time job**, especially if you have a good attitude towards your work, show attention to detail, have good time management skills and are reliable. These are skills that all employers want. Sometimes, they are prepared to train you on the job if you show reliability and a 'can do' attitude.

PUTTING TOGETHER THE PIECES

SOME PRACTICAL STEPS

Give yourself plenty of time to research all the options open to you.

Did you know…

…that by studying subjects that really interest you, you may discover possibilities you hadn't realised were available? For instance, did you know that by taking certain science courses, you could end up doing research for a company developing new products in the food and beverage industry? Ever thought of working for a winery or a company developing specialist gourmet chocolate?

1. **Make sure you have the right entrance requirements for the course you want to take.** Check this out with your careers adviser. Entrance to diplomas and certificates varies according to the institution. Visiting the institutions' websites for entrance guidelines is another option.

2. **Make sure you don't concentrate on one subject at school and neglect the others.** You need to have sufficient numbers of credits from several subjects. Don't spread yourself too thinly either, by taking so many subjects that you only get a few credits in each. Again, check out the entrance requirements and make sure you know what the requirements are.

3. Take opportunities to gain experience and skills while you are still at school by being involved in sport, drama, music, organisation, student government and/or part-time jobs.

4. Take every opportunity to find out about careers by going to events such as careers expos, careers evenings at school and open days at universities and colleges.

5. Check out the prospectuses for universities and colleges – they may give you new career ideas. Most of them have toll-free numbers and will mail you any brochures or material for free.

6. Compare courses and costs but don't sacrifice quality for price – in the long run it's not worth it.

7. Remember it is not only the subject of your qualification that is significant, the skills you acquire while studying are important too. They are skills that will be useful throughout your life.

8. **Don't get too specific too soon. Choose a qualification that gives you a broad range of skills.** For instance, if you gain a diploma or certificate in one specific area of business, it limits you. If you do a general business degree first, it keeps the options open and the skills are more general. If you want to specialise, do it after you complete the first qualification.

9 Check out the job listings in newspapers and websites such as www.seek.com.au, www.seek.co.uk, www.mycareer.com.au and www.monster.com. **Find the jobs that look interesting to you and see what qualifications they require.**

10 **Find out what qualifications and skills you will need by doing some research** – such as phoning the kinds of companies you would like to work for and talking to people in the same industry. If you know what company you want to work for, check with their Human Resources department to see what qualifications they require.

11 Talk to anyone you know – family, friends, neighbours and others – who are doing the kind of job that looks interesting to you. Find out what they like and don't like, the pros and cons of the job.

Last but not least, **enjoy your time at school**. Don't become anxious about what you will do when you leave or what your career will be. If you put the effort in and do the homework of checking out the possibilities, you will be fine. And don't forget, you are not setting yourself in concrete – there are ways to change the course of your career. *Keep your options open and look forward to the choices you will make about your future.*

ENJOY BEING THE AUTHOR OF YOUR OWN STORY!

BIBLIOGRAPHY

Career Development and Systems Theory: A New Relationship by Wendy Patton & Mary McMahon, 1999, California: Brooks/Cole Publishing Co.

The New Careers: Individual Action & Economic Change by Michael B.Arthur, Kerr Inkson & Judith K. Pringle, 1999, London: Sage Publications

The Future of Career edited by Audrey Collin & Richard A. Young, 2000, Cambridge: Cambridge University Press

Authenticity and Health: An Existential Perspective, MA Thesis by Heather McAllister, 1999, Auckland: The University of Auckland

FURTHER READING

For Nietzsche and Sartre:

Standford Encyclopedia of Philosophy
http://plato.stanford.edu

For Heidegger:

The Internet Encyclopedia of Philosophy
www.iep.utm.edu

For further resources, please visit www.wilkinsfarago.com.au.